BODIE: GOOD TIMES & BAD

GOOD TIMES & BAD

Nicholas Clapp

PHOTOGRAPHY BY

Will Furman

SUNBELT PUBLICATIONS, INC.

San Diego, CA

Bodie: Good Times and Bad

Sunbelt Publications, Inc.
Copyright © 2017 by Nicholas Clapp
All rights reserved. First edition 2017

Cover and book design by Kathleen Wise
Project management by Deborah Young
Printed in South Korea

Please direct comments and inquiries to:
Sunbelt Publications, Inc.
P.O. Box 191126
San Diego, CA 92159-1126
(619) 258-4911, fax: (619) 258-4916
www.sunbeltpublications.com

20 19 18 17   4 3 2 1

Contemporary photography by Will Furman unless otherwise noted on pages 108–109.

Library of Congress Cataloging-in-Publication Data

Names: Clapp, Nicholas, author.
Title: Bodie : good times & bad / Nicholas Clapp ; photography by Will Furman.
Description: First edition. | San Diego, CA : Sunbelt Publications, Inc.,
 [2016] | Includes index.
Identifiers: LCCN 2016040006 | ISBN 9781941384268 (softcover : alk. paper)
Subjects: LCSH: Bodie (Calif.)--History--19th century. | Bodie
 (Calif.)--Moral conditions. | Bodie (Calif.)--Biography.
Classification: LCC F869.B65 C44 2016 | DDC 979.4/48--dc23 LC record
available at https://lccn.loc.gov/2016040006

Dedicated to the memory of Bodie's hardy men, women, and children.

They put up with a lot.

Stalked by swaggering shootists, their sagebrush town

earned a reputation as a violent, hell-bent corner of the desert West.

Passing through, Mark Twain said he would have it no other way.

Virtue versus vice made for exciting times.

Indeed, he wrote, "It was a plain wonder how man carried on under such circumstances."

Table of Contents

A note on the book's color photographs:

Many of these appear to be double exposures. But they're not. Rather, they're actual scenes—of window reflections. Photographer Will Furman calls the technique "Inside-Out." It requires just the right time of day and lighting, just the right angle, and just the right lens. Befitting Bodie, the resulting images are illusory—and haunting. Visit Bodie and you can experience them firsthand.

A note on veracity:

When news was dull or slow, Western newspapermen—and frontier folks in general—delighted in making things up. Accordingly, in the following account, imagination may have had a seat at the table—and slyly dealt a hand or two.

As the shafts, drifts, and stopes of Bodie's mines are dangerous and off-limits, current-day images of underground workings are from similar mines, as nearby as possible.

Bodie

MAP OF BODIE

1 "Angel of Bodie"
2 Rosa May burial site
3 Old Morgue
4 Miller home
5 Metzger home
6 Dolan home
7 Methodist Church
8 Bill Brown home
9 J.S. Cain home
10 Jail
11 Bodie Bank (*vault survives*)
12 Sawdust Corner Saloon
13 Assay Office
14 Barber shop & Sam Leon Saloon (*adjoining*)
15 Lottie Johl home
16 Boone Store
17 Bodie Morgue
18 Miner's Union Hall
19 Odd Fellows I.O.O.F. Hall
20 Post Office (*in same building as 19*)
21 Masonic Hall
22 U.S. Hotel
23 Wells Fargo Office
24 Courtroom
25 Occidental Hotel
26 Firehouse
27 Wheaton & Hollis Hotel
28 Swazey Hotel
29 School
30 Standard Mill Complex

Chinatown

Old Tailings Pond

Bonanza St.

King St.

Prospect St.

Union St.

Geiger Grade

(Bypass Road)

Fuller St.

Green St.

Main St.

Bodie Creek

Standard Ave.

Wood St.

To Bodie & Benton Railway Depot

Cemetery

0 100′ 200′ 300′

Source: Bodie Historic State Park

Surviving Structures
Long-gone Structures

"A fearfully and wonderfully bad place."[1]

———◦◦◦———
[1]*Bodie Daily Free Press*, Jan. 7, 1880.

PROLOGUE:
Bodie's Bluff

IN THE SUMMER OF 1859, Wakeman S. Bodey, said to have been a sallow, slouchy fellow, was prospecting east of California's Sierra Nevada Mountain when he spied an injured, limping rabbit. He pursued it through the high desert sage, only to have it disappear down a burrow. He hesitated for a moment, considering that he was up a draw by the name of Rattlesnake Gulch. But then hunger got the best of him, and he plunged his arm up to his shoulder—but failed to catch the creature. No luck, no dinner.

Instead, he beheld a handful of quartz, glittering with gold! Cause to exclaim, "Pay dirt at last! And I came a hell of a way to find it."

That's the legend. Whatever the reality, he'd struck it rich, and was off to purchase supplies—only in his return to be caught in an early November blizzard. Prospector friends were to find his body in the next spring's thaw, wish him well in whatever lies beyond, and set about seeking a share of his treasure.

Therein began a fitful decade, and life in a hardscrabble camp little different than a hundred or so others scattered like dice across the deserts of the Far West. Its name? A sign painter lettered "B-O-D," but was unsure how the name ended. He guessed, incorrectly, "B-O-D-I-E." The population was no more than forty or fifty souls.

In 1863, J. Ross Browne, an itinerant mining reporter and artist, paid a visit:

The rugged cliffs along the road cropped out at every turn like grim old castles of feudal times. We reached the base of a conical hill, surmounted by a range of reddish-colored cliffs, very rough, jagged, and picturesque, a capital-looking place for a den of robbers or a gold mine.[2]

---

[2]This and the quotes that follow are from J. Ross Browne articles in *Harper's New Monthly Magazine*, August & September, 1865.

"COME ON, SIR."

A gold mine it was, though of uncertain worth. Atop Bodie Bluff, Browne asks if he might have a look around. Venture underground.

The mine's boss cheerily replied:

"Certainly, Sir, suit yourself; only the ladder's sort o' broke in spots, and you'll find it a tolerably hard climb down; hows'ever. I'll go ahead and sing out when I come to the bad places."

Browne hesitated. Then down he went.

The descent was perilous, hand-over-hand.

The ladder, it seemed had been broken by a blast of rocks; and now there was to be another blast. We retired into a convenient hole about ten or a dozen paces from the deposit of Hazards' [gun] powder. The blast went off with a dead reverberation, causing a concussion in the air that affected one like a shock of galvanism; and then there was the diabolical smell of brimstone. A mass of the ledge was burst clean open. My friend was charmed by the result. He grasped up the blackened fragments of quartz, licked them with his tongue, held them to the candle, and constantly exclaimed: "There! Sir, there! Isn't it beautiful? Did you ever see any thing like it?—pure gold almost— here it is—don't you see it?"

J. Ross Browne didn't "see it"; the rock was anything but beautiful. And he had the good sense to be on his way.

In the very same year, a fellow by the name of Leland B. Stanford was on the scene, to float over a million dollars in stock in his self-acclaimed Bodie Bluff Consolidation Mining Company. The woodcut certificates were impressive, if inaccurate—and beyond that, disingenuous. They placed the mine in the town of Aurora, which was not in Mono County, California, but rather across the border in Nevada. And they portrayed a beehive of a bluff sprouting eleven "consolidated" mines and pocked with an astounding two miles of tunnels (or so Stanford claimed).

With the ink hardly dry, a dubious expert advised Stanford that in his considered opinion there was unlikely to be gold deeper than 200 feet below the surface, prompting Stanford to sell his entire Bodie holdings for $500, and move on to less sketchy enterprises, among

A promised cornucopia of coin (left), signed by Leland B. Stanford (right).

them the transcontinental Central and Southern Pacific Railroads, and the university bearing his name.

Listless years were to follow. An earnest, hardworking African-American—"Uncle Billy" O'Hara, known locally as "the colored capitalist"—worked a Bluff mine, came up empty-handed, and sold out to partners Peter Eshington and Louis Lockberg.

Alas, this was not to Uncle Billy's relief, but rather to his regret, for upon sinking a hapless 120 foot shaft, Eshington and Lockberg were on the verge of abandoning the mine when a lower level caved-in—and laid bare a rich deposit of sugary, gold-bearing quartz.

Suddenly and from the corners of the Far West, a rush was on! A printer hauled in a press; his newspaper exalted:

> Gold—But a few short months ago Bodie was an insignificant little place, now she is rapidly growing in size and importance, and people are crowding in upon her from far and near, and why? Because of the rich discoveries of gold—yellow, glittering, precious gold.[3]

Come spring, a telegraph line was strung, and a message went out:

> Bodie sends greeting to the mining world and proclaims her gold mines are the most wonderful yet discovered.

[3]*Bodie Weekly Standard*, Nov. 7, 1877.

Belmont, Nevada boasted a grand courthouse and shady lanes, but in the late 1870s, not much else.

Good-by, God

THE GLORY DAYS OF WESTERN MINING were over, or so it appeared. The easy gold of California's mother lode had been blasted from the earth, as had the bonanza silver of Nevada's Virginia City. Honest work was scarce; hard times were at hand.

There had been hopes for a next "big thing." But alas, a score of promising prospects had fizzled.

The Nye County seat of Belmont, Nevada, had appeared an exception, with an estimated population of 4,000 or more working its nearby mines and mills. But now the ore was playing out, with the cost of extracting anything further prohibitive.

More than others, the town's Brotherton family would have felt the pinch. Though little is known of them, father Lee appears to have been seriously injured, whether in a farming or mining mishap is unknown. The family, though, appears hardy enough: young wife Essie, near-grown son Harry capable of wielding a hoe or pick, and indeed, Lee able to work in a mercantile or hold down a desk job in a mine.

They would have been typical of folks lighting out for Bodie, for them no more than a few days away.

Down front in a photograph of the Brotherton family are little Effie and her sister Viola, five and nine years old. They're of the age of a little girl legendary in Bodie lore. On the eve of her family's departure for the booming town, she was said to have gathered her dolls, that they might join her as she knelt by her bed, her prayer to conclude with a somber,

"Good-by, God; we are going to Bodie!"

Belmont's Episcopal church (as the town emptied out, moved to Manhattan, Nevada).

Word was that the camp was hard-bitten, desperado-ridden.

Getting wind of the girl's farewell to the Almighty, the *Bodie Weekly Standard* reported that, oh no, that wasn't what the girl had in mind. Not at all. Someone had gotten the punctuation wrong. What she surely said was…

Good, by God, we are going to Bodie!

That little girl could have been from Belmont or as far away as San Jose, or she may not have existed at all. In any case, the likes of the Brothertons would have bid farewell to friends, screwed up their courage, and looked over their shoulders as they passed their town's hilltop church.

It would, indeed, be years before the citizens of Bodie would get around to raising a house of God.

What roads there were over to Bodie—lonely, rutted tracks, dusty or muddy depending on the season—could well have had a family seeking comfort in the words of a familiar hymn.

Come, oh partners in distress,
Good comrades in the wilderness.
A while forget your griefs and fears
And look beyond this vale of tears.

Somber wayside cliffs echoed morose verses, in time to give way to other sounds. The clop of hooves, the imprecation of mule skinners, the rumble and squeak of wagon wheels.

A family hailing from Belmont would join a swelling throng. There'd be men, women, and children, their earthly belongings packed into buckboards and wagons. Stagecoaches would rattle by "filled with passengers from deck to keel. Sixteen is an average load, but as a stagecoach is like a can of sardines, there is always room for just one more."[4]

Ahead, they believed, lay good fortune, prosperity, a better life.

Dating to the fall of 1877, Bodie had regular stage service.

[4]*Bodie Weekly Standard*, Sept. 18, 1878.

A newcomer's view of Bodie, with its bluff dotted with mines and mills.

Bodie had wide streets, and yet they were crowded with twenty-mule freight and lumber teams—and folks with high hopes and often not much else.

Bodie's streets would echo with the shouts of teamsters piling up goods—from prams to coffins—outside of hammered-up shops that "grow as if by magic… Bodie merchants are doing good business. Trade is coin; jaw-bone don't go."[5]

Bodie was, round the clock, a lively town.

From time to time, up and down Main Street, curious crowds would gather, amused by a range of incidents. There could be a heated argument between a bartender and a bounced drunk, a hair-pulling spat between rival harlots, or as old timer Frank Wedertz recalled,

One that attracted an interested crowd was a battle between a Chinaman and an Indian. The Indian had snowballed the

Chinaman and the latter fought back. As the Indian was attempting to cut the Chinaman's queue, officers arrived and halted "the rape of the lock." Then, a large family of gypsies arrived and set up camp south of town. It was not long before one of them had a knockdown argument at Boone's Corral.[6]

At the close of that lively day, "a number of the ladies caught their husbands in the company of some Bonanza street women [prostitutes] and wrecked the establishment."[7]

[5]Daily Standard- News, Dec. 11, 1880.

[6]Frank Wedertz, *Bodie: 1859–1900* (Bishop, California: Chalfant Press, 1969), p. 15.

[7]Bonanza Street was to become the home and workplace of Bodie's "syrens of easy conscience."

Outbound teams carried mail—and newly poured gold ingots.

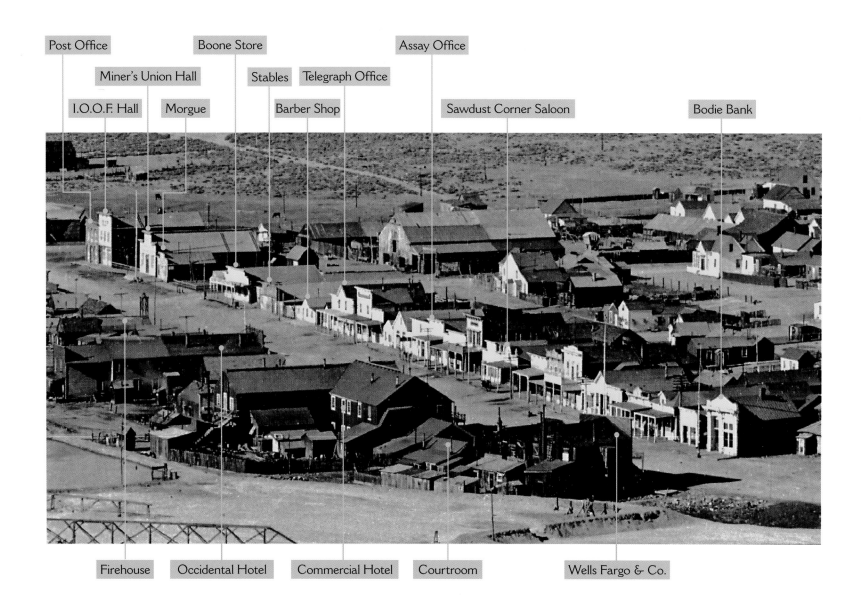

Post Office

Miner's Union Hall

I.O.O.F. Hall   Morgue

Boone Store

Stables   Telegraph Office

Barber Shop

Assay Office

Sawdust Corner Saloon

Bodie Bank

Firehouse   Occidental Hotel   Commercial Hotel   Courtroom   Wells Fargo & Co.

From a vantage point on Bodie Bluff, the town's Main Street and a sampling of its landmark buildings. A balance of the rest are saloons.

Men and boys (but no women) gather for a group portrait on a boardwalk fronting the Commercial Hotel.
As with the fellow with his back to the camera (left of center), their stances and expressions vary.

Despair

Confidence

Uncertainty

There was a tradition for families or individuals arriving in the likes of Bodie, be they Brothertons, DeChambeaus, Garcias, Petrallis, or Fongs. They would put on a good face and celebrate with a square meal, even if short on coin. Accommodating them, the town offered a choice of Callahan's Can Can Restaurant or the Bon Ton Eating House, or even a table at the tony Grand Central, where:

> The commodious dining hall was not always patronized in accordance with its elegance. One evening a rough looking teamster stalked into the dining room and sat down at a table. He kept his hat on. The polite waiter asked him what he would have for an entrée. "Damn yer ongtre!" he said, "bring me some dinner."[8]

Seeking employment, the Brothertons would have had a number of options. Lee was good with numbers, and God knows here there were numbers—dollars by the fistful—

[8]Wedertz, *Bodie*, p. 68.

A welcome dinner at the Occidental Hotel.

to keep track of. Young Harry could do well in the mines; they were paying as much as four dollars a day.[9] And Essie could be in demand as a waitress or even a cook. The Lafayette Restaurant boasted meals prepared by ladies only.

The sooner the better, the Brothertons would seek a home of their own, and put down roots. It didn't have to be much or fancy—just homey, with rhubarb plants and petunias on a window shelf, and cutlery, cookware, and curtains from their old place in Belmont.

[9]In twenty-first century dollars, eight hundred dollars or more a week.

If little else, miner's shanties were refuges from Bodie's frequent storms and snows.

It was chilly, even inside. Year-round, Bodie has fewer than thirty days and nights when the temperature didn't dip below freezing.

Cherished companions.

Food was canned, but also fresh.

For newcomers in 1878 and years to come, this wasn't rural New England or even the Midwest—with as a reminder of this the oft profane, sometimes angry shouts rising from the proliferating thirst parlors down on Main and Green Streets. And from time to time, shots rang out in the night. There were encouraging signs, though. An Odd Fellows Lodge was chartered, its mission "to improve and elevate every person to a higher, nobler plane." As well there were earnest Rebekas, upright Masons, and Elks (also upright, though familiarly "Masons who drank").

No church, not yet—though talk of one.

All had their chores. Even so, there was a nagging question: Considering its rowdy repute, was Bodie fit for kids?

15

At an elevation of 9,000 feet, here was "the highest school in California."
Its boast of "young scholars" was wistful—with boys frequently out of control and up to no good.

To accommodate an initial ten children, Miss Belle Moore had opened a school, only to have it burned to the ground by a disgruntled delinquent. But then, Bodie citizens took over a boarding house, the Bon Ton, pronounced it a school, and installed a cupola and bell to round up boys and girls, cited as "young scholars." Soon they numbered a hundred and fifty.

A one-time Bodie scholar would recall:

Mining camp life had a very unfavorable effect upon boys as they grew toward manhood; the example set by their elders could not have been worse, and the doors of every kind of dissipation were wide open. The good women and the girls, on the other hand, lived their lives apart, respected and even revered. I recall with deep satisfaction the sweet, modest girls with whom I went to school.[10]

As to the bad-boy behavior he questions, it wasn't just dipping pigtails in inkwells and sassing teachers, offenses that were curtailed by ruler raps to knuckles. It was seventeen- and eighteen-year-old hoodlums skipping school and down at the intersection of Green and Main hassling girls, caging drinks, and picking fights. All the while dishing insults and swearing a blue streak.

[10]Smith, Grant H. "Bodie, Last of the Old-Time Mining Camps," *California Historical Society Quarterly* 4 (March 1925), p. 79.

To an extent, Bodie girls were a civilizing force, though not immune to gossip and shared secrets. Note the Dixie Queen tobacco can, the lunch pail of the day.

Teacher's desk. Respect was hard-won.

In a newspaper ad, the school sought a teacher "big enough and brave enough" to right the situation, which brought to the fore a Mr. McCarty, who promised to, if he had to, tend to business with a six-shooter. He didn't have to. He instead wielded a long-handled stove poker, no mind if it was painfully hot. Recalled a fellow teacher, "He sure did battle those toughs."

One by one, they quit school and order was restored, at least in Bodie's schoolhouse.

A schoolyard stick 'em up. By all accounts, Bodie's girls were not to be cowed, and held their own—
even to the point of mimicking the town's lawless element.

Beadle's Dime New York Library

COPYRIGHTED IN 1888, BY BEADLE & ADAMS.

ENTERED AT THE POST OFFICE AT NEW YORK, N. Y., AT SECOND CLASS MAIL RATES.

Vol. XXXIX. | Published Every Wednesday. | *Beadle & Adams, Publishers,* 98 WILLIAM STREET, N. Y., May 16, 1888. | Ten Cents a Copy. $5.00 a Year. | No. 499.

TWILIGHT CHARLIE THE ROAD SPORT

OR,

Sulphur Sam's Double.

A Romance of the Wild Lands of the Yampah.

BY J. C. COWDRICK,

AUTHOR OF "RAINBOW ROB," "KENTUCKY JEAN," "BLUE-GRASS BURT," "GILBERT OF GOTHAM," "THE GIANT CUPID," "BROADWAY BILLY" STORIES, ETC., ETC., ETC.

CHAPTER I.

"HANDS UP!"

FAINT but clear rung out the silvery tones of a cornet, waking the echoes of the mountain wilderness with one of Foster's most plaintive airs, the notes reverberating from hill to hill and dying away at last in the valleys and canyons.

It was in Northwestern Colorado, in the wild region north of the Yampah River and near the Little Snake River whose united waters go to form the majestic Colorado.

The time was twilight—that mystic hour

IT WAS SULPHUR SAM. WHOOPING AND YELLING HE DASHED AWAY UP THE VALLEY AT BREAKNECK SPEED, FIRING HIS REVOLVERS AS HE WENT.

One wonders: Was there something in the high desert air that prompted an obliviousness to acceptable behavior? Bodie was to increasingly—even enthusiastically—tolerate violence, be it casual or deadly. Readers were amused, hardly outraged, when a paper editorialized:

> To be sure here is something of a shooting gallery, but what are we to do? Inexpensive recreation is needed, six shooters are of no account unless used, and coffins will warp if left in the undertaker's room.[11]

It may well have been that Bodie was in the throes of a condition in which grown men, certain ladies, and even children were affected not by the desert's air or altitude, but by its vast, windswept, high-lonesome landscape. *Intimidating, it was. Made a person feel small, tiny even, of no account.* Add to this a daily challenge to survive, if not make something of yourself. Faced with this, a number of individuals were to take comfort in colorful names, pack pistols and Bowie knives, and make general, even fatal nuisances of themselves—*so that they might be somebody, feared and in a backhanded way, respected.*

Do anything to be recognized.[12]

It didn't help that currently popular nickel and dime novels added fuel to the fire as they chronicled—and all but celebrated—the exploits of such outlaws as Three-Fingered Jack, Snap-Shot Sam, Dick the Dead Shot Dandy, and Twilight Charlie the Road Sport, a highway and byway bandit.

In a Twilight Charlie rant:

I'm bad. I'm a warhorse from the hills and a fighter from hell. I'm a mile wide and all wool. You hear that?

I run on brass wheels.

I'm a cyclone out of the howling wilderness. Want to hear me howl? Wa-a-agh! Yow-yow-oh!

Don't tread on me unless you want a whole cageful of wild animals turned loose on you. Them's me![13]

[11] *Bodie Daily Free Press*, June 10, 1881.

[12] This was proposed and analyzed in Wilbur Shepperson's classic, *Restless Strangers* (Reno: University of Nevada Press, 1970).

[13] J.S. Cowdrick, *Twilight Charlie the Road Sport* (New York: Beadle & Adams, 1882), p. 2.

Dime novel desperado Twilight Charlie.

Bad Men from Bodie

IN THE BOOM YEARS of 1877 to 1880, a journey to or from Bodie was at one's peril.

There was a desperado logic—a cracked reasonableness, if you will—to laying in wait and holding up Bodie's stages. Especially if they were outbound. There was gold in the bluff rising from the town that every few days was cast into ingots, and on its way to

In Bodie scores were often violently settled. In the late 1870s, shootings were said to have been a nightly occurrence, with the next morning a druggist or undertaker discovering a dead body on his doorstep. "A man for breakfast," they called it.

23

With a lack of authentic images of stage robberies in California's high deserts, this will have to do: an image of a camp-to-camp stunt to sell typewriters, here a *Smith Premier* clutched by the salesman in the duster.

San Francisco. The road out traversed barren, unpopulated country—with ample opportunities for a surprise ambush. As a bonus, there were the wallets, purses, and watches of well-heeled passengers.

Not only that. The timing was such that desperados could lighten the load of a westbound stage, then an hour or so later reap the spoils of an eastbound one.

Bandits were familiarly known as "road agents," and such were their depredations that teams of Bodie horses would slow and stop where their stages had previously been robbed, to patiently await the deed. Indeed, the holdups were initially relatively tame affairs, short on bravado and long on the business of robbery followed by a hasty retreat up remote desert canyons.

An exception came when in the dead of night, one L.E. Short single-handedly stopped and robbed an incoming stage, and come dawn, was tracked by the law in the person of an Officer Harrington and three savvy Indians. Unexpectedly, they were pinned down by a hail of gunfire, killing an Indian.

This Wells Fargo handbill described the shooter as "bony; pretty broad shoulders; full beard and moustache; steps very long when walking; drinks and smokes; wore black sack coat with two buttons behind; black hat very slouchy; rather green and gawky."

In short, a newly minted murderous, if clumsy, bad man.[14]

> ☞ To Agents Wells, Fargo & Co.—Don't Post, but place these Circulars in the hands of Officers and discreet persons only.
>
> ## ARREST
> ## Stage Robber and Murderer!

[14]The fate of road agent L.E. Short is unknown.

In mid-February of 1878, mayhem was to descend the surrounding hills and stalk downtown Bodie. Gunfire pierced the wintry air as James Blair traded shots with John Bresnan, with both men forthwith "flipped into eternity" (as the expression went). This was cause for the first of a sad series of entries in an oversize leather-bound, gold-tooled volume: *The Mono County Register of Deaths.*

Date of Record.		NAME.	Nativity.	Cause of Death.
Years.	Months. Days.			
1877	Aug 4	Bryant, Geo Porte	California	Measles
"	Dec 9	Binaile Moise	Canada	Pneumonia
1878	Feb 23	Bresnan, John	Nova Scotia	Gunshot wound
"	" "	Blair James	Topsell (Maine)	" "
1880	Jan 2	Brandon Patrick	Ireland	{Falling to bottom of shaft}

A reckoning of Bodie scourges:
measles, pneumonia, gunshots, and a mine accident.

Additional face-offs were chronicled in Bodie's newspapers.[15] Items included:

On Main Street, Bill Deegan and Felix Donnelly dueled at long range, "with nine shots exchanged. Not even a bystander was killed."

Rough-and-Tumble Jack and an opponent coolly drew and unloaded their guns at a range of two feet, and astonishingly, neither was fatally wounded. Jack repaired to the nearest bar, while his adversary, despite a shattered arm, reloaded his gun by holding it between his knees, with the consequence that Jack was forthwith bidden "to answer the toot of Gabriel's horn" (in an expression of the day).

Pat Shea and John Sloan blasted away at each other during a masquerade ball. Bystanders counted fourteen bullets. "Neither of these crack shots suffered a wound, and luckily, neither did any of those counting the rounds."

A stage set for Main Street mayhem, without and within.

Not to be slighted, two cat-fighting "syrens of easy conscience" were pitched out of a saloon, head first through a glass door.

These and further colorful confrontations need to be taken with a grain of salt. Reporters relished penning them; they sold papers. Nevertheless, one thing appeared to be the case: Bodie's bad men were bad shots—to the extent that their town—and their aim—was derided in rival Candelaria, a mining camp to the south. Its paper called Bodie not only a "Shooter's Town," but "Bad Shot Gulch."

[15]According to research by historian Sue Silver, there are at least twice as many burials in the Bodie cemetery as entries in the *Mono County Register of Deaths.* Did officials in the quiet county seat of Bridgeport distance themselves from the mayhem up the hill in Bodie?

In the Wheaton & Hollis Hotel, a surviving restaurant, pool hall, and bar.

By night and in foul weather, the antics of Bodie's "blood and thunder men" moved inside.

Every thirst parlor, boarding house, and dance hall had its stories—and characters. There was Red Roe, fond of quoting Shakespeare and the Scriptures, but mean and given to murderous tears. Portrayed in a Bodie paper, "He called for a cocktail of lava, lightning, bitters and gin, and got it. All the women of the town locked themselves in. He went on the war path, and he made ponderous blows on lunch counters that made dishes dance. He was a holy terror."[16]

And there really were "such melodious characters as Big Eared Sam, Rattlesnake Joe, Bad Mike, and Snooks."

If this sounds like bluster out of a dime novel, a measure of blame lies with one E.H. Clough, a Sacramento newspaperman, who may (or may not) have visited Bodie and witnessed (he claimed) one Washoe Pete leaping upon a billiard table and shouting:

"Here I am again, a mile wide and all wool. I weigh a ton and when I walk the earth shakes. Give me room and I'll whip an army. I'm a sand storm mixed with a whirlwind. I'm bad from the bottom up and clear grit plumb through."[17]

[16]*Bodie Daily Free Press*, Nov. 30, 1880.

[17]*Sacramento Bee*, Oct. 12, 1880.

E.H. Clough noted that if a rant climaxed with a burst of profanity, there'd be hot lead whistling through the air. "If he didn't swear when he drew then he was not the real thing. This oath of the Bad Man from Bodie is like a cheerful warning of a rattlesnake."[18] And with this last line, Clough initiated a wooly Western legend, that of

THE BAD MAN FROM BODIE

He became an archetype, prompting newspaper accounts and riveting readers from San Francisco to New York City. And unfortunately for Bodie, the image was to draw would-be shootist, come to town to strut and swear, and make their mark. They would then move on to venues further afield, there to be admired by little kids and plague lawmen who had little need for an "angel from hell" thumping a bar "in need of the necessary." Or the carrying-on of a "curly wolf with wool in his teeth."

In the local and national repute of "the Bad Man from Bodie," gritty reality and dime-novel fantasy were hopelessly confounded.

But maybe, just maybe, Bodie wasn't such a bad place after all. Records are sketchy, but in the reputedly bullet-ridden year of 1879, there were likely more deaths from mining accidents, pneumonia, cholera, and the like. Suspect were newspaper statements that "hardly a day goes by without a killing." Or: "A day without a killing is newsworthy."

[18]*Bodie Daily Standard-News*, Oct. 16, 1880.

Likely the case: when they were bad, Bodies' bad men were very bad, and drew undue attention as actors in their misbegotten, larger-than-life melodramas. But then again, as reported, they were generally bad shots, with good reason. Through drunken bloodshot eyes in a smoky, ill-lit saloon it was hard to get a fix on an opponent. Then there was the question of guns. To accommodate long-barreled "self-cocker" Colts, a scattering of bad men wore holsters. Most, though, preferred small pistols tucked in waistbands and concealed in coat pockets lined with velvety buckskin to prevent a hammer from snagging in mid-draw. In an exchange of insults or a hot-under-the-collar fistfight, they'd offer an element of handy surprise.

A diminutive Derringer.   Popular in Bodie, a British Bulldog.

Unfortunately (or fortunately if you were on the receiving end) these weapons were of necessity short barreled—as little as two inches—and wildly inaccurate. Drawn at any distance, as in a street-strutting shoot-out, they were all but hopeless, and in crowded saloons they were unreliable, be they jostled in a soused crowd or grasped in the unsteady hand of a bibulous bad man.

There you have it: bad-shot bad men, possessed in the words of the *Bodie Daily Standard*, by "some irresistible power that impels us to cut and shoot each other to pieces."

As a farewell to all this, consider a Friday afternoon, that of January 17, 1879.

Harry Dugan was to trudge from his boarding house on down to the Phillips and Moore's Saloon, there to pull a long night's shift as bartender.[19] A dozen men, including mean, loud-mouthed John Muirhead, lined the bar. A year ago, Muirhead had his forearm blown off in a mining explosion, then after being fitted with a hook hand, returned to work, only to slip and fall eighty-five feet down a mine shaft.

Looking down Main Street, Bodie. Every door or so, another saloon.

[19]No such saloon appears in Bodie documents. Perhaps it was a saloon with a differing name, owned by one J.R. Phillips and a fellow Irishman named Moore (whose wife was to shoot herself later in the year).

Hard-edged bartender Harry Dugan didn't care for sour John Muirhead or his woes. So what.

As night fell, and the evening wore on there would be tired jokes, often dwelling on the saloon's Lightning Whiskey, said to be "a concoction of old boots, scraps of iron, and snow slides."

"Naw, naw," a barfly could have disputed, "Dugan there serves up a mix of turpentine, Perry Davis pain-killer, Jamaica ginger, and pepper sauce. Kinder a cross 'tween a circular saw and a wildcat. Whatever it is, takes just a couple of

snorts to craze a man."[20] Dugan had to agree. He had only to look around. What was he doing catering to these deadbeats? Muirhead, particularly Muirhead.

At this point, the saloon's piano man could have hocked a spit, swiveled his stool, and struck up a ditty. Tension would have slacked. But not for long.

A prostitute and her john now waltzed into the saloon, ordered a round of drinks, and asked a few acquaintances to join them. Without

[20]*Bodie Daily Standard*, Feb. 27, 1879.

being invited, Muirhead barged in and reached for a drink. The lady of the night protested the intrusion, said she only drank with friends. Taking offence, Muirhead advanced with, according to a next day's paper, "the evident intention of assaulting her." At which Harry Dugan rounded his bar and clubbed the belligerent miner, sending him reeling out the saloon door, but not before he was heard to growl, "I'll get even with you."

Come two o'clock in the morning, John Muirhead returned, asking for the man who had struck him. Harry Dugan didn't hesitate; he answered, "If you were struck in here, I'm the man that done it." With that, Muirhead drew a revolver, took aim at the bartender, and opened fire. Two rounds narrowly missed him, several more were wide of the mark.

A barrel was tapped, spouting a stream of ale. A surprised bystander had a cigar shout from of his mouth, all but an inch-long stub.

Dugan, in the meantime, had drawn his own revolver and returned the fire, a round grazing Muirhead's head, others driving him out of the saloon and shattering the glass of its front door. As the one-armed miner retreated into the night, Dugan calmly offered the man who'd had the cigar shot out of his mouth a new one. He noted, "Stub of the old one's not long enough to light."

The sum damage of eighteen shots fired? A keg of ale, a cigar, a broken window, and a ricochet wound to Muirhead's head. This didn't help the reputation of Bodie men as bad shots, even if considering the difficulty of hitting an intended target in a smoky saloon, crowded with drunks and bewildered bystanders, chock-a-block with gaming rigs and layouts.

Those who knew John Muirhead allowed he was a mean spirited ruffian, "anxious to make a record." *To be someone, no matter his repute.* Last heard, he'd taken leave of Bodie, drifted to Colorado, and in some remote camp or other, had been shot dead.

"Here's to old John. Remember John, John Muirhead?"

31

Thou Shalt Not!

A railroad was never to connect Bodie with the outside world. Transport was by horse, whether ridden or harnessed to carriages or wagons.

A baseball team happy to be bound for a Sunday out-of-town game, be it in Bridgeport, Bishop, or even Virginia City.

$\mathcal{C}$OME SUNDAY, the one day a week Bodie's mines were shut down, there were choices. Recovering from a Saturday night toot, a fellow could sleep in; a family could be off to a picnic down by Mono Lake; or with a sigh, one could tack up for a short ride to church and an opportunity to salve one's conscience. Stay on the right side of the Lord.

Church?

For twenty years and then some, Bodie hadn't gotten around to building a church, with both Methodist and Catholic services held in the Miner's Union Hall. It was now that a Mr. Walker from Reno sought to establish a place of worship for Bodie's devout, with the curious rationale that escalating deaths from pneumonia were beneficial "in the way of directing the inhabitants toward the consideration of the probability of the hereafter."[21]

It was agreed that "a general improvement in morals would not be out of place."[22]

---

[21]*Reno Weekly Gazette*, Nov 20, 1879.

[22]Cited in Wedertz, *Bodie*, p. 50.

In late 1882, the bell of a newly completed Methodist church rang out, summoning the faithful, such as they were.

Gaze through a pointed gothic window, if you will, and imagine a service led by the Reverend F.M. Warrington. They were never that well attended. With Sunday a miner's one day off, the last thing he needed was a hellfire fulmination, popular as they were with preachers of the day. (After all, didn't a miner labor "ten feet from hell"?)

There would have been a hymn offering consolation in a fearful world:

When drooping pleasure turns to grief,
    And trembling faith is changed to fear,

The murmuring wind, the quivering leaf,
    Shall softly tell us, Thou art near.

All would then be seated to listen, if listlessly, to a reading, something along the lines of Psalm 26's, "Lord Gather not my soul with sinners, nor my life with bloody men…" And then Warrington might offer an extended homily, a variation on his lamentation that in Bodie, "We are cast into a sea of sin, lashed by lust and passion."[23]

---

[23]Penned in a letter to Mrs. Thomas D. Penfield, Jan. 25, 1881.

As to the congregation, the front pews would have been the preserve of Bodie's rich and near rich—and righteous given to, as they felt appropriate, passing judgment on their perceived inferiors. Whatever lesser folk might have been in attendance would have been in pews to the sides and rear. In particular, these would include the families of miners who in their calling were lucky to survive more than a few years underground, and who were old men at the age of thirty-five.

There was a telling word for them: *dispensable.*

As the service rambled on, Bodie children would squirm and stifle yawns. Or gaze at the back of the groomed heads of folks up front they didn't recognize—gimlet-eyed mine owners and portly capitalists in from San Francisco or even New York, the moneymen reaping the rewards of Bodie's boom. From there, a kid's attention might wander to the framed Ten Commandments painted on oilcloth and hung on the wall behind the preacher. (They've since been stolen; so much for No. 8).

Indeed, a kid might wonder: How was their Bodie measuring up?

Let's see, beginning with No. 1: "Thou shalt have no other gods before me." Considering that the words "Bodie" and "godforsaken" often shared the same sentence, townfolk's fingers were crossed that He even cared.

As to the rest of the lot, there would be abysmal marks for No. 3: "Thou shalt not take the name of the Lord thy God in vain." Nor could much could be said for No. 7: "Thou shalt not commit adultery," considering the frolics a few blocks away on Maiden Lane, recently renamed Bonanza Street.

And there was No. 10: Thou shalt not covet…thy neighbor's ox, nor his ass." But what about his gold? Jeezle-beezle, who *didn't* covet gold?

Skipping back to No. 6, what about "Thou shalt not kill?" A big goose egg on that one, considering Bodie's surfeit of self-proclaimed "curly wolves" and "angels from hell." But wait, did they have a corner on villainy? What about the proper and righteous up front, under the reverend's nose? Might they stink a bit, considering their astounding disinterest in the safety of their mines, and a resulting, ever-increasing number of funerals, many within the walls of this very building?

The Fortuna Vein

The surviving gallows frame of the Red Cloud Mine. Whether by vertical shafts or horizontal drifts (tunnels), the camp's doughty miners sought the riches of Bodie Bluff.

IN A HEADLONG QUEST for Bodie's riches, the lack of safety devices and procedures was appalling. With out-of-town capitalists not satisfied unless they made two to five percent *a month* on their investments, mine superintendents were pressured to shore up workings only when absolutely necessary, skimp on pumping down air, and with the exception of a single mine, the Champion, skip installing safety cages (in use elsewhere for a decade). As well, they'd rush the handling of Giant Powder—dynamite. A miner would pack holes while his "highballing" partner continued to drill nearby, with the risk that his partner could swerve a hole, and in the words of an old-timer, "that would be final."

Miners flocked to Bodie from as close as Belmont and Virginia City, Nevada, and as distant as Wales and eastern Europe. They were well aware that mining was "an uncertain, hazardous business, a hunt for something in the dark." (*Bodie Weekly Standard*)

An early Bodie miner, Daniel Butler hailed from Indiana.

Butler's daughter Marietta. Her son was the first child born in Bodie.

A day shift assembles at the mouth of the Bulwer tunnel of the Standard Mine.
Working ten hours a day, six days a week, they'd spend more time underground than in the light of day.

Or lighting a fuse, a man could run like hell, but not fast enough if the fuse was "a runner." Or quickly returning to shovel ore freed by a blast, a miner could be victim of a "steamboat," a dud that had smoldered and not exploded, with a horrible loss of hands and eyes, if not life.

October 9, 1879, was a particularly black day in Bodie's mining history. On a shift change, nine men boarded a cage to descend the Tioga shaft. A lax hoist engineer failed to clutch its reel of cable to its engine. The cage plummeted 520 feet, "flipping its occupants into eternity."

And there was unfortunate Elrod Ryan, who slipped and fell 450 feet, yet nevertheless had the presence to sing out to the men working at the bottom of the shaft, "Look out below, I'm coming!"

Yet the search for fortune and fame in this high lonesome town went on, on the part of capitalists—and as well, willing miners, who against their better judgment believed themselves caught up in a grand adventure, man against nature, even as it wore them out. And to this end, there was encouraging news—jubilation!—when the shaft of the Bodie Mine, at 436 feet, cut a vein of "exceeding richness." As the price of stock in the mine rocketed from $6 to $69 a share,

Long abandoned workings.

The goddess Fortuna in easterner
John Gast's *American Progress*, 1872.

there was the question: Could this be a "true fissure vein" welling from the depths of the earth, as at Nevada's Virginia City, making one and all—well, at least some—rich beyond imagining? Verily, a second Comstock Lode!

An eastern newspaper proclaimed:

Gold Galore!

A New Bonanza Discovered, with Millions In It.

What to call this? The mine's management settled on the "Fortuna Vein," after a Greek goddess oft-cited and popular in the Far West.

With Christianity's God not interested in championing the search for gold (actually, quite the opposite) she was a logical, if pagan choice. In a period painting, Fortuna favors miners trekking West, thoughtfully reeling out telegraph line (coiled in the crook of her right elbow) so that they could relay their success to loved ones back East.

Down the vein went. Gold-bearing quartz, ranging from two inches to two feet wide. Three times it was lost in a sideslip, only to be regained, and at a depth of 600 feet widen into—a bonanza!

At this point, in the excitement of pursuing the Fortuna there was a temptation. It had to do with the fact that, working a rich vein,

Abovd: A single candle saw a miner through a shift. Below: As good as it gets.

a miner's shovelful of ore could be worth more than he'd make in a year. So what was the harm in helping himself to a sample? *High-grading* it was called, and it was justified by a popular notion that "Hadn't the Lord put gold in the ground, and didn't it belong the anybody who found it?"[24] If a fellow was up on his Bible, specifically Deuteronomy 25:4, didn't the Lord ordain, "Muzzle not the ox that treadest the corn"?

Miners would tuck choice ore under their caps, slip it their pockets, tuck it in their boots, stash it in a lunch bucket—to put food, delicacies even, on their tables; outfit their wives in fine dresses; buy cute togs for little ones; and to set foot in a favorite saloon and shout a traditional warning that a fuse had been lit: "Fire in the head!—drinks on the house!" An 1879 article in the *Bodie Chronicle*, entitled DECIDEDLY RICH, allowed that,

> When a mass of ore is thrown down, a man can scrape up enough loose dust to enable him to get away with $5,000 in his lunch bucket in three days. What a glorious place that big hole in the ground is for a light-fingered gentleman to work in![25]

[24]Ella M. Cain, *The Story of Bodie* (San Francisco: Fearon Publishers, 1956), pp. 60–61.

[25]*Bodie Chronicle*, Nov. 8, 1879.

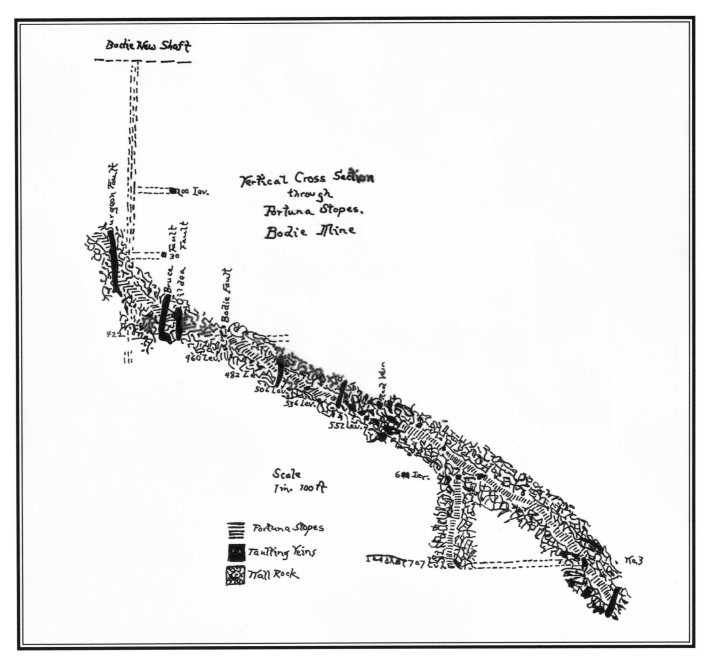

A mining engineer's cross section of the Fortuna's bonanza.

A Bodie miner shares his underground drift
with a nervous wife and daughter.

Now a buried and forsaken world.

A caved-in shaft, and in a shallow pool of underground water, a "widow-maker" drill. Introduced at the time of the Fortuna vein and spewing rock dust, it added the crippling cough of silicosis to pneumonia as a pox afflicting Bodie miners.

But alas, at the end of 350 glorious feet, what was to be Bodie's biggest bonanza—praised as "collosal"—was to fork, fracture, and give out. In the regretfully terse words of its mine's annual report, "Its departure was abrupt…the Fortuna was immediately impoverished."[26]

Surely, though, there were still riches at depth, for weren't they pursuing a "true fissure vein"? Down and down the Bodie Mine's shaft plunged. There was fleeting hope as fragments of Fortuna quartz were struck, only to miserably pinch out.

At 1,200 feet, the search was abandoned, and the mine's lower workings were left to decay, crumble, and collapse.

As in time would all of Bodie's mines—and the town itself.

[26]*Bodie Consolidated Annual Report #4*, 1883, p. 14.

Bodie stock, soaring, falling, ever-manipulated by greed-bent industrialists. Ultimately sinking to pennies a share.

Snowbound

OME FALL, with inky clouds cresting the Sierra Nevada Mountains to the west, a first snow would swirl down Main Street, and Bodie folks would repair to one or the other of thirty-five saloons and a toast to "the last rose of summer, left blooming alone." And down the bar, there'd be a rejoinder, "Oh! who would inhabit his bleak world alone?"

They would. And they'd make the best of the winter to come.

For days at a time, thermometers would read 30° to as much as 40° below zero.

47

Storm-racked houses would shudder and creak. Wind-driven snow would find it way through their every seam and crack.

There'd be fifteen-foot drifts—burying Bodie, isolating its men, women, and children from the outside world.

Undaunted, they dug their way out.

On news of a sleigh full of letters, townsfolk would gather at Bodie's post office.

In the face of adversity, they entertained themselves. Most everyone played an instrument, be it a kazoo or a Sears Roebuck roller organ. They sang, they sawed and tooted. And there was a joy in flowers, kept by the stove and lovingly tended.

Florence Molinelli had a fine voice, whether singing opera or popular songs of the day; Jack Dolan was a rowdy, knee-slapping comedian; John McDonnell, everyone agreed, was an eloquent Shakespearean who could quote "the bard by the yard."

There were dances. Indeed, the Miner's Union Hall's floor was mounted on springs, so that folks could twirl and sashay the night through, from the warmth of one pot-bellied stove over to another.

With saloons offering round-the-clock warmth lacking in homes and boarding houses, Bodie folks drank. No surprise, and often to excess. Which in the case of an inebriate named Midson may have been both his woe and his salvation. Expelled from a saloon, he toppled into a snow bank and fell asleep. When discovered the next morning, he was frozen solid, or at least appeared so, with not a sign of life. Nevertheless, friends plunked him by a stove with the hope of thawing him out. And indeed, apparently preserved by the alcohol in his veins, he

Song and dance lifted snowbound spirits.

blinked awake—to ask for a drink. A doctor on the scene commented that an ordinary man would have died from exposure, to say nothing of pneumonia.

Severe cold spells, it was agreed, were "real pneumonia weather," with 1879 a dreadful year. Miners were susceptible. In the course of a winter shift, in workings dank and choked with rock dust, there at least was warmth, in the range of 60° to 65° Farenheit.

But then there would be a rapid ascent to the sub-zero surface, and an invitation to the condition and disease. Further, it was said that if pneumonia didn't fell folks, the town's dicey doctors surely would. With news that a medical man was off on his annual hunting trip, a journalist concluded that "it was the only time of year in which the good doctor didn't kill anything."[27]

There was refuge in gallows humor. Jim Townsend of the *Bodie Miner Index* was to report:

> A local man was buried last week. 'Tis said that he had asked his wife, with a wan smile, "I do think I could eat a bit of the ham I smell cooking." "Oh no, honey dear," she replied, "you can't eat that; that's for the wake."

In the argot of the day, "many a citizen answered the toot of Gabriel's horn."

Even so, Bodie's citizens persevered, resourcefully and cheerfully so, even in the face of dull thuds periodically trembling the earth and rattling windows—Giant Powder touched off to loosen frozen earth and provide graves for coffins crowding the cemetery's nearby "dead house."

On a cheerier note, they gathered for ice-skating parties on Bodie's frozen mill ponds. And there was the slapdash fun of an impromptu snowball fight.

[27]Wedertz, *Bodie*, p. 109.

Note the ladies in the second floor window, rooting for the woman in the long dress.

Sleigh rides toured Bodie's surrounding hills.

From atop Bodie Bluff, five sports swoosh down into town.

In newspapers beyond the camp, as off in San Francisco, there were reports of Bodie folk sporting "snowshoes." And these for a time were assumed to be clumsy, rawhide-laced trapper footwear. They weren't; *they were skis*, up to twelve or more feet long, and "doped" with locally brewed wax, with ingredients ranging from pine pitch to spermaceti. Bodieites organized ski clubs, with one challenging another.

Due to their length—which increased their speed—the skis couldn't be turned, or braked by forming a "V." The only way down was straight down, and the only way to brake was to indecorously sit on a pole dragged between a contestant's legs.

Skiers were clocked at up to ninety miles an hour, with runs often ending in cartwheel crashes.

As early as age four, children were fitted with "snowshoes."

If favored by a full moon and a cloudless sky, nearly everyone in Bodie—men, women, and children—would at night wend their way up Green Street to a roaring bonfire high on the flank of Bodie Bluff. They'd warm themselves, then strap on their skis and down they'd go.

Cheered by nips from flasks, they'd trek back up, fly back down.

Again and again, whooping it up, having the time of their lives.

The modest residence of J.S. Cain.

Flush Times

Snowmelt heralded Spring—and in 1879 the arrival of John Stuart Cain, destined to become the town's leading light. He was an "industrialist," but not in the sense of out-of-towners given to quick profits, manipulating stocks, and not caring a whit about the place or its people. Rather, Cain cared for Bodie, and stood by his town in good times and bad for sixty years, before reluctantly moving on to San Francisco to care for his ill wife, Delilah.

Whether the place be wicked or tame, thronged or near-abandoned, Cain loved Bodie.

Knocking on the door of Cain's Park Street home, a visitor was ushered into a Victorian world of chenille drapes, lace curtains, lavish wallpaper, velvet carpets, and a clutter of elaborately wrought furnishings—footstools to grand pianos.

A dapper J.S. Cain.

Married to Ille, short for Delilah.

Cain was not what you'd expect looking at photographs in which he appears to be either stern or strangely startled. Neither was the case. Rather, he was astute and easygoing, given, in fact, to elaborate practical jokes that ranged from a fake stage holdup to sweet potatoes magically sent over a phone line.

Venturing to Bodie at the age of twenty-one, he was to parlay captaining a little ship into, eventually, owning the better part of the town. The ship was the *Rocket*, a tiny puffer-belly steamer nudging lumber barges across nearby Mono Lake, their timbers essential to shoring up cave-in prone mines. It wasn't long before he owned a few of these mines, constructed mills to process their ore—and was party to a lease that discovered a fragment of the famed Fortuna vein, and before the agreement expired, take out $90,000 in three months. He then bought out the Bodie Bank, and ultimately the better part of all Bodie. And throughout his days, he'd cherish a dream: to tap the lost Fortuna's strayed treasure. According to his daughter-in-law Ella, he would pray for this, "Dear Lord…"

J.S. Cain's Bodie is hauntingly preserved. Light filtering through the dusty panes of many a home illuminates a gallery of nostalgic, evocative scenes—tattered tableaus of a once-vibrant frontier life, in which folks busily wallpapered and decorated their homes—at once modest and opulent—plumb in the middle of nowhere. In Bodie.

A glimpse of Bodie's faded past.

Below: with its reclining sofa and cozy fireplace, the living room of timber and railroad man Tom Miller, his wife, and young son.

A dining room where glasses were raised and hopes shared.

A game once won and lost.

Accounts
to be kept.

Valuables to be
safeguarded.

A fine, freighted-in bed in the home
of mill foreman Henry Metzger.

The timeworn, bereft home of the Dolans,
their menfolk county sheriffs.

To dream of gold, endless gold.
Once the bedroom of miner Bill Brown.

A well-dressed Bodie mother and child. Mrs. Julia McKinley Burnett's expression is enigmatic. Lucky to fare well in a rough-and-tumble town? Dreaming of a life far away? Hopeful? Regretful?

Bodie's women dressed well and were no strangers to vanity.

A chair for perusing *The Bodie Standard* or the *Daily Free Press*.[28]

A chair for settling accounts or tallying mining stocks.

A chair for a shoeshine in the barber shop adjoining Sam Leon's saloon.

[28] Readers might be puzzled by an apparent abundance of Bodie newspapers. Eighteen are on record! In reality, there were far less, as with mergers and acquisitions, they changed their names.

Our Nation's Birthday

Boone's Dry Goods.

$\mathcal{C}$OME SUMMER, the four roads into Bodie—from Dogtown, Bridgeport, Aurora, and Mono Lake—would be clogged with wagons wallowing in mud, and bearing everything from lace-trimmed white frocks to cast-iron mining machinery.

As a tonic to cabin fever and its privations, Bodie's folk would crowd the camp's newly stocked mercantiles.

If they were of a mind to do so, Bodie's women could dress as fashionably as any fine ladies in Virginia City or San Francisco.

A Bodie lady's clothing trunk.

Belles of Bodie, their identities unknown.

There'd be fresh fruits and vegetables from the Bridgeport and Carson valleys. Exotic comestibles would range from Point Reyes oysters to imported Dutch herring, from Vermont maple syrup to Russian caviar.

Coffee ground to order.

From Corona cigars to Venard's mustard, near anything you'd want.

Come every July, there was a grand opportunity to connect a remote high desert town with cities and states across America. With a number of Bodie men trading pickaxes for rifles, the nation had weathered and survived a devastating Civil War.

The time was at hand to parade down Main Street, to nobly orate, to let off steam, to proclaim patriotism!

A gentle but firm advisory.

On the stroke of midnight of the eve of a July 4th, the steam whistles of Bodie's twenty-three operating mines shrieked and echoed across its hills—fanfare for a rowdy three-day celebration of Our Nation's Birthday.

At 4:30 AM a brass band serenaded the town from the Belvedere Iron Works, their repertoire featuring "Hail, Columbia" and "The Red, White, and Blue." Then, anyone able to sleep through this would awaken to discover Main Street decorated with flags and festoons of bunting. Not only that: aspen, willow, and poplar trees had been carted into town and lashed to posts the length of Bodie's boardwalks—only in one year be blown over by "a very strong wind, causing the dust to rise in clouds, cause for a great deal of profanity."

An Indian mom and her kids in town for the festivities.

At 10 AM, a parade would step off to the cacophony of one band, then another, then another. Veterans of the Mexican and Civil Wars proudly marched, as did Odd Fellows, Masons, and Elks. Atop their shiny brass engines, hook and ladder firemen showered a cheering crowd with twist-wrapped candies.

Curious Paiutes.

A cheery geezer.

A popular float—a "Car of State filled with youth and beauty," little girls bearing thirty-eight pennants, one for each state.

Leading the girls' hundred-yard footrace.

To the right, the finish line of the men's three-legged race. As well there'd be a sack race, an egg race, and a fat man's race.

Afternoons would feature contests. In five minutes, what double-jacking team could drill the deepest hole in a boulder? Who'd be the first to shovel a carload of ore? There'd be a greased pole to climb, and "a Grand Wrestling Match" at the Bodie hay yard. And there were races.

With mines fielding rival teams, Bodie cheered the newly popular sport of baseball—as well as the venerable sport of horse racing.

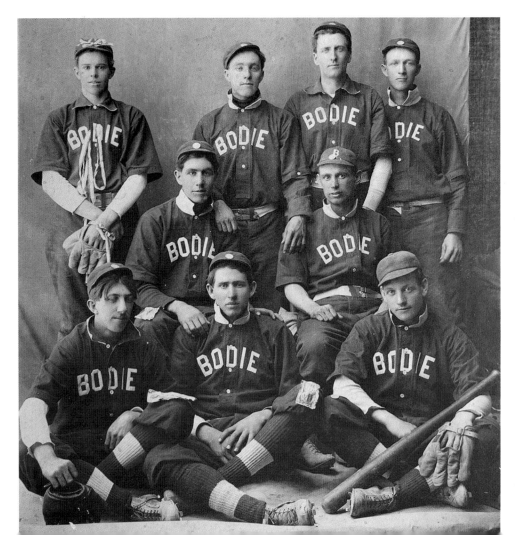

"Small boys," a reporter noted, "were out with cracker and bomb, making all the noise possible; frightening horses, timid ladies and prowling dogs." And masked *"Horribles"*—nobody knew who they really were—roamed Bodie, heaping abuse on the self-important, the pompous, the rich. Somersaulting and cartwheeling, they were given to satirical processions.

They started out on their predatory march, and a grotesque looking crew they certainly were. At the head, mounted on a crazy mustang, came their leader, his office that of the grand Bombshell. Next, the band, blowing tin horns, ringing bells, playing triangles and beating gongs, and making a most discordant noise. Among the motley throng was noticeable his satanic majesty in a suit of red, as usual up to all sorts of mischief. Humpty-Dumpty wobbled around with a game leg. The Dutchman was a holy terror.[29]

How many boys could pile on a long suffering burro?

[29]This and the following quote are from the *Bodie Weekly Standard*, July 10, 1878.

A contingent of Bodie Horribles.

A Horrible orator addressed a gathered crowd,

Fellow Horribles, Loafers, Bummers, Four-time Losers, Cross-road Sports and Ragged Companions! Celebrate to your heart's content, but above all things, I implore you do not forget the great and grand principal of our order—"To do unto others as you darn please, without allowing them to return the compliment."

This sentiment, it might be said, would have been no surprise in hard-case Bodie.

And this being Bodie, its Fourth was punctuated by explosions. In 1880, one George Hanscon laid an old anvil on "a heavy charge of powder and then set fire to a fuse. The thing did not work as fast as Hanson thought it ought to, and he went back to see what the matter was when the explosion occurred, bursting the anvil and throwing pieces in every direction," including that of said Hanscon (severely burned, lucky to retain his eyesight).

Come the next year, a cannon firing a sunset Fourth of July salute was to "burst from 'butt to muzzle.' Half of it went sailing high in the air; the other fragment smashed through the gun carriage. Since no one was injured, the explosion provided a grand finale for a splendid Day."[30]

That night a gala dance was held in the Miner's Union Hall, attended by young men bent on courtship, older folks kicking up their heels, and out-of-control Horribles.

Midnight, and everyone poured out into Main Street, to witness to fireworks arcing heavenward from atop Bodie Bluff and exploding in the night sky. Then it was back to dancing until dawn.

[30]*Bodie Daily Free Press*, July 6, 1881.

A Bodie tot, his dog, and his world.

The Bodie & Benton Railway

The brakeman, fireman, and engineer of the Mono.

OR A TOWN FOND OF DIVERSIONS, yet cut off from life beyond its barren hills, November 8, 1882, was a welcome day. A new whistle was sounded, not that of another mine, but of a diminutive 2-6-0 Mogul locomotive, one of a trio—the Mono, Inyo, and Tybo—hauled in to freight in lumber cut on the south side of Mono Lake, and raise not only new buildings, but to prop open Bodie's ever-expanding, ever-hopeful warren of shafts and tunnels

Further, it was promised, the tracks of the Bodie & Benton Railway would reach the sleepy ranching town of Benton, and a promised connection to one or more transcontinental railroads. Imagine! All the way by rail—from little Bodie to the shores of the Atlantic.

As the little engines whistled and chuffed, a newspaper editor relished the racket and professed relief, given that "the town had become terribly quiet, one never heard a gun go off any more…".

The Inyo. For machines with personality, it was hard to beat the robust little engines
that crisscrossed the deserts of the West. Beloved for their gumption, forgiven for their quirks.

It wouldn't be long before the B & B Railway—affectionately the "Born & Booming"—would offer excursions the length of its line to the logging outpost of Mono Mills. It would be "All aboard!" for up to 400 passengers riding as many as seven swaying flatcars.

To the squeal of brakes and sparking wheels, the train would switchback down the twelve miles and nearly 2,000 vertical feet to the sagebrush flats encircling Mono Lake. Engineers wisely held their top speed to 15 miles an hour. To go faster would risk, on tight curves, the little but heavy engines jumping their narrow gauge rails. Nevertheless, it was an exciting, even giddy ride, particularly when the tracks ran fifty feet above the ground over a 260 foot trestle. Close by the shore of the awesome lake—to Mark Twain, "a giant, solemn, sail-less sea"—there would be a stop at Warm Springs, and its camp for crews pushing the line on to Benton and, hopefully, a connection to all of America. Here, a fork in the line had the train heading south, not east, and a relatively easy run to Mono Mills.

The view north from Mono Mills. Bodie lies in the far blue hills beyond Mono Lake.

Mono Mills now and, below, back then.

Bound for Bodie, sawed planks and beams were piled at the base of skids.

At the end of their three and a half hour journey, Bodieites would dine and whet their whistles at Gilcrest's general store, whose proprietors "threw open their establishment from garret to cellar—more particularly the cellar."[31] And after a satisfying lunch, the floor would have been cleared for dancing to the strains of a band that had ridden the rails.

But then, for many, there would be the best part: "To see the woods…The sweet odor of pine and the aroma of fresh sawdust reminded one he was a long way from Bodie."[32]

———— ·«●»· ————

[31]Quoted in David Myrick, *Railroads of Nevada and Eastern California* (Berkeley: Howell-North Books, 1962), p. 310.

[32]Ibid., p. 309.

Along footpaths and in shady glades, flowers bloomed. Birds called and twittered; deer grazed.

As shadows lengthened, holiday-makers would offer their Mono Mills hosts a rousing "Three cheers and a tiger!" Of one such occasion, it was reported that "No social event in Bodie had ever been more thoroughly enjoyed."

They would then be on their way back to Bodie's barren, nowhere hills.

Some, though, would stay on, the next day hiring a team and wagon that would transport them west across primitive roads winding up into the Sierra Nevadas.

Mono Mills folks on the porch of Gilcrest's general store.

The Sierras have been called "the gentle wilderness" —
temperate and welcoming, a contrast to daunting Bodie.

Bodie folks camping, possibly within the boundary of present-day Yosemite National Park.

For a magical time,
Bodie was a world away.

Keepsakes.

There was refuge and solace in the Sierras that would comfort the life of one Lottie Johl—a woman of Bodie legend. Accounts of her character and life wildly differ. A farm girl from Iowa, she had fled a bad marriage and headed West, there to be called "Naughty Lottie,"[33] likely an allusion to being an "accommodating woman" working Lulu's Dance Hall in Candelaria, a Nevada camp rivaling Bodie. Whatever the case, Lottie was said to be a decent enough woman, of merry and gentle disposition. "She was an attractive lovable girl, with soft hazel eyes, and light curly hair, and seemed to be smiling all the time."[34] She loved to dance, and off in Candelaria caught the eye of bachelor Eli Johl, a well-liked butcher and the proprietor of a local hotel.

Eli believed her a wonderful woman. He respected her, loved her. He proposed.

They got a proper license, exchanged rings, and were married on the fourth of July, 1881. And together, they were on their way to Bodie.

[33]*Reno Evening Gazette*, Nov. 8, 1879.

[34]Ella M. Cain, *The Story of Bodie* (San Francisco: Fearon Publishers, 1956), p. 108. With its "artistic license," her further account of the life of Lottie Johl is, at the very least, suspect.

Eli & Lottie Johl's new home.

Here, they'd have a new life.

Together, they would enjoy a five-room home Eli purchased for Lottie on Main Street. There were trips to Bodie's mercantiles to obtain the finest in furnishings, from velvet carpets to reputedly the best sideboard and piano in Bodie. Proud of the result, they planned a celebratory party. They invited friends and acquaintances. With Eli carving choice cuts of meat, Lottie prepared a fine dinner.

No one came.

Or so it was said.

But then, contradicting this, there were newspaper accounts of Lottie's popularity, how she was the belle of many a dance. "Mrs. Johl was the most richly dressed lady on the floor…a gorgeous, golden glittering costume…and Eli Johl, as Prince Carnival, was gorgeously attired—the most richly dressed male character on the floor."[35]

It would only be natural, then, if this display could have irked a strata of the prim and proper women of Bodie and prompted them to shun, even scorn Lottie. And cause the couple to keep to themselves

[35]Cited in Nick Gariaeff, *Discovering Bodie* (Gilroy, California: privately printed, 2010).

Lottie Johl.

As it may have graced her home, a surviving painting by Lottie Johl.

in their fine home. It would have been an increasingly lonely life, apart from Bodie's social swirl, such as it was.

But then, encouraged by Eli, Lottie took up painting, with her favorite subject the Sierra Nevada mountains, their snow-capped peaks, wildlife, lakes, and streams. Lottie pined for that world, an enchanting wilderness, as the crow flies but fifteen miles—and a world away—from treeless, bleak Bodie.

A few years and Lottie took sick, and died.

There was said to be the question of where to bury her. Should a woman with Lottie's questionable past be interred within the cemetery overlooking the town, in sanctified ground, shoulder to shoulder with Bodie's righteous citizens? Absolutely not, many said. But others weren't so sure, considering that, for many a year, Eli and Lottie had lived a faithful and loving life.

A compromise was reached. She could be buried just—but only just—inside the cemetery's fence.

For years, every Memorial Day, Eli Johl would raise a canopy over Lottie's grave and decorate it with flowers and red, white, and blue bunting. He'd sit by his love until shadows fell, and it was time to trudge on home.

Long gone—the round-the-clock thunder of the Standard Mill's ore-crushing stamps.

A whirring, shuddering array of shafts, wheels, belts, and gears.

On the Hill

Amalgamation tables, where gold was freed from crushed ore.

B Y THE EARLY 1880s, Bodie's bad men had moved on, as had much of its population, sinking from an estimated 7,000 to 9,000 to perhaps 500 souls. Of its thirty mines, only two—the Bodie and the Standard—were doing well. Gone were the heady days when a single mill could refine a $10,000 bar of gold bullion a day.[36]

Yet there was hope for the future. Ever-zealous in his quest for the extension of the Fortuna vein, J.S. Cain would buy out the nearby Midnight Mine. On a practical level, he would outfit mills with vats of sodium cyanide, effective in processing low grade ore that previously had been relegated to Bodie Bluff dumps.

[36] Worth $400,000 or more in today's dollars.

Detail of a five stamp battery. As the output of Bodie's mines dwindled, one by one its stamps were silenced.

An apparently witless mill worker perched on a vat of deadly cyanide.

In its latter days, the Standard Mill was the scene of a crime "that beat anything for daring that was ever pulled off in, or around, Bodie."[37] A run of bullion was white-hot and ready to be poured when the sole hand on duty took a break and strolled down into town for a spot of dinner. A footpad who'd been keeping watch forthwith snuck into the mill's retort room and resumed the job where the melter had left off. He methodically poured the sizzling bullion into molds, hosed them with cold water, and hustled back and forth carrying the bars

[37]Ella M. Cain, *The Story of Bodie* (San Francisco: Fearon Publishers, 1956), p. 72.

In the Standard Mill's retort room—a rush of liquid gold to glint a visitor's spectacles.

down the hill to where he'd dug a hole to bury them in. As he exited for the last time he was spied by Standard watchman Joe Best. Shots were exchanged and both men were wounded, though neither fatally. Collared and hauled into Bodie's Justice Court, the miscreant pleaded guilty, and was offered the option of leaving town and never returning. As long as they didn't kill anyone, the town was chronically easy on those who filched gold, be they high-graders or out-and-out thieves.

Commandment No. 10 to the contrary, who in Bodie *didn't* covet gold and "thrill at its sight"?

Throughout boom and bust, mining was consistent in one thing: its perils, with the handling of Giant Powder—dynamite—at the top of the list.

Back on the night of July 10, 1879, a Mrs. Shay, wife of a hoisting engineer, was on her way to her husband's mine, his dinner bucket in hand and their child crooked in her arm. Her route took her close by the Standard Mine's storage bunker and its two tons of dynamite—that at 7:30 PM violently exploded. She was knocked to the ground, unconscious. Her child was hurled ten feet and her arm broken.

The explosion was tremendous, flattening several homes and boarding houses and shaking the buildings the length of town. Breaking windows, dashing clocks and crockery, showers of rocks and boulders rained down, crushing roofs, shattering walls.

In a state of panic, townsfolk rushed outside to behold an immense cloud of black smoke and fire mushrooming high in the twilight sky.

The Bodie region had in the not-so-distant past experienced volcanic eruptions. Many at first thought this to be the next.

Fire bells rang, mine whistles shrieked, and hundreds ran up the hill to dig out survivors and mourn the dead. Seven men were instantly killed, with several soon to die in a makeshift hospital and morgue set up in the Miner's Union Hall. Among the forty injured: "Alex McGregor, head injured and three ribs broken…Thomas Murphy, eyes out and arm fracture…Hugh McMillan, shoulder blade broken, internal hemorrhage, may not live."[38]

A tragic day for Bodie, with more to come.

[38]As reported in Wedertz, *Bodie*, p. 194.

With no photographs taken of the 1879 Standard blast, this gives an idea of what it was like—
the last of three subsequent explosions and conflagrations to lay waste to Bodie.

Bodie's morgue.

Undertaker Ward's parlor of death.
He also offered a selection of for-sale
chairs, tables, and sideboards. Furnishings
for the quick; furnishings for the dead.

On the wall. For some, a sole mourner.

"What man shall live and not see death?" Psalms 89:49.

The Methodist church's pump organ would wheeze. Its congregation would hang and shake their heads. And there was an oft-sung funerary dirge—"Poor Effie Is Dead!' Its closing verse:

Step lightly—breathe softly
    Speak not aloud;
She lies there so meekly
    In her snow-white shroud!
Her eyes, once so beaming,
    Their lustre have shed—
She lies as if dreaming,
    But O! she is dead!

Might this, in coming years, be an elegy for Bodie?

By Night

A late afternoon summer storm—echoing a pervasive gloom at the turn of the twentieth century.
At hand: a time when "Coin is scarce and folks feel blue."

Girls and a gent on a summer eve. A row of prostitute's cribs—"the line"—continues on down Bonanza Street.

WEST FROM UPPER MAIN STREET lay Maiden Lane, known as Virgin Alley, ultimately renamed Bonanza Street.

Now, with Bodie's golden dreams fast fading, there was little hope for a bonanza future.

The Bodie red-light district had been a world unto itself, with its own dance halls, saloons, and even mercantiles. On occasion, girls in need of finery or on an errand would venture to Main Street, as did Kittie Willis, "a dashing damsel from a 'palace of folly and sin.'" At the

Wells Fargo office, she was to bump into a Mademoiselle Albisu, a rival on the line. Reported the *Bodie Daily Free Press*:

> On meeting their eyes met and flashed fire. Mlle. Albisu made a terrific dash at her enemy and gave her a stinger under the right ear, which left a red mark. This was followed by a right-hander to the check, which had the effect of knocking off a spoonful of powder and paint." Kittie returned the blow, and spectators, relishing the action, were on the verge of making bets when the altercation disappointingly ended.

Then it would have then been back to Bonanza Street, and a life that had an element *zip-boom-hurrah-bang*, but more often was hard and demeaning, with escape and relief in strong drink, and opium offered in nearby Chinatown dens.

Back at her crib, a girl would stare silently into the night.

"Fair but frail," Bodie's harlots, as flowers of the desert, fleetingly bloomed and fast faded. Their colorful nicknames, bestowed by sarcastic customers, masked the sad, sometimes suicidal stories of the Beautiful Doll, Bull Con Josie, the Castilian Cyprian, French Joe, Madame Moustache, Peek-a-boo Patten, and Big Bonanza No. 1.

And there was Rosa May.

A late arrival in the midst of an economic decline that had many ladies of the night on an outbound stage, she had pursued her profession in Carson City and in Virginia City, to then settle on Bodie in the early 1900s—with accounts of her stay a tangle of reality and melodramatic fantasy. Did a client's largesse cut Rosa May in on the treasure of the Fortuna vein? Doubtful. Did she do sufficiently well to tour Europe and return with a wagonload of French finery? Possibly. In any case, she had somewhere acquired Bonanza Street's fanciest red lantern, and hung it from the eave of her brothel.

Rosa May had a paramour, Ernest Marks, a Main Street bartender. Nevertheless, she appears to have very much liked and even enjoyed her clients. She'd listen to them, their stories and woes. She'd help them write letters home; she'd even darn their socks. When a latter-day pneumonia epidemic gripped Bodie, she was said to have gone from one miner's cabin to the next, to console and nurse some back to health, some not. "Many a time she closed tired eyes that would never open again."[39]

Until the day came when she herself contracted dread pneumonia. And in a few days died.

With her sad, honorable demise, a rift long dividing Bodie was to widen—of the proper and pious opposed to those deemed wayward and fallen. Saints versus sinners.

At stake was where to bury Rosa May. *Not* in the cemetery up the hill's hallowed ground, "decent" folk insisted in a fit of censorious prudery, its extent mirrored in a widely read book in which a Dr. J.H. Kellog wrote, "I have thought deeply on the subject, and have no hesitation in saying that attribute much of the vice and immorality now prevailing to the insidious influence of the waltz."[40] The waltz? Blamed in a shooter's town?

In Bodie, was murder to be shrugged off, yet the kindness of a harlot condemned?

A younger Rosa May. Was she the proverbial "whore with a heart of gold"? Accounts generally agree that, indeed, she was.

[39]Cain, *Bodie,* p. 62.

[40]In a *Ladies Guide to Health*, to this day on the shelf of J.S. Cain's parlor.

Bodie's cemetery, with Rosa May's grave over the fence on down the hill.

It depended on what in the Bible a citizen favored, forgiveness or vengeance.

In the end a compromise was reached, and Rosa May was borne on a sled to where gunfighters were buried in unmarked graves, and laid to rest in a plot just outside the cemetery's encircling fence. Whatever words were spoken and by whom is unrecorded, but they could well have been along the lines of a *Bodie Morning News*' observation: "Whatever else may be said of the class known as fallen women, they are always to be found more generous, kind and forgiving than in the case of their more virtuous sisters."[41]

And in place of a hymn, there might have been, one would hope, the like of a song of the time that asked, "Do not scorn her with words fierce and bitter…"

[41]*Bodie Morning News*, Sept. 9, 1879.

After a rare rain. Left to right, the adjoining Post Office and I.O.O.F. Hall, the Miner's Union Hall, and Bodie's morgue. Below, the Wheaton & Hollis Hotel.

The Standard Mill, of late its sole occupants a pair of horned owls who,
startled by a night watchman, winged out through a window, showering their haunt with glass.

A road below the now abandoned Standard Mill angled off to the Nevada camp of Aurora, with the last house to the left the home of little Fern Grey. As a grown-up, she was to recall:

> My dad told me a tale of a miner with a white mule, the pair working an old mine across from our house. The miner and the mule died tragically in the mine, and if anyone approaches it, the white mule will appear and keep them out. As a kid, it scared the daylights out of me, and I never went near the mine. I suspect that's why he told me the tale—to keep me out."

This is but one of many stories now befitting a town of unlatched doors swinging on rusty hinges, of abandoned and perilously leaning buildings, of the odd drunk enraptured by spectral lights.

Soon enough, all Bodie would be a ghost—a ghost town.

EPILOGUE:
Bodie, 1932

With their tripod and camera to the right, a crew in from Hollywood visits the Sawdust Corner.

"THE DAYS OF OLD, THE DAYS OF GOLD" were gone but not forgotten. There was a nostalgia for the place, and cause for many to motor back to their youthful home.

They were warmly greeted. The Sawdust Corner Saloon, a Bodie fixture dating to its early days, welcomed customers.

In the Sawdust Corner, backbar glasses would still tremble, as up the hill handful of men dynamited pillars left to support the roofs of old workings, a dangerous proposition. "Gophering" it was called.

And a few doors on up Main Street, from ten to two, J.S. Cain opened the doors to his Bodie bank, even if for days at a time there were no deposits, no withdrawals. In the words of a visitor,

He was a refined little old gentleman and wore a stiff collar and blue serge suit. His grey hair and his rather sorrowful eyes showed that he was living in the past. His life was now only the imagination of what it had been.[42]

[42]C.C. Keely, 1925 typescript in collection of Bodie State Historic Park.

The Bodie Bank. Its owner J.S. Cain was convinced that deep down, the gold was still there.
There'd be a rush; he'd greet and accommodate the crowd.

Parked by the cemetery.

On the afternoon of June 23, 1932, a Bodie tot, not yet three and playing with matches in a derelict building behind the Sawdust Corner Saloon, lit a piece of dangling wallpaper, and watched in awe as flames shot up the wall. His mother rushed to the scene, caught him up. Said he, "Look what I done!"

A fire bell rang. Men raced down the hill to man pumpers and hoses, but to no avail. Unmaintained, Bodie's water lines were clogged with dirt and rocks, and were no match for the challenge. Building after building burned to the ground. For a while, it looked as if the Bodie Bank might escape the blaze. As a precaution, J.S. Cain asked his two visiting granddaughters to gather what they could. Helen returned with a bucket of gold specimens taken from a display case; Ruth clutched a *Webster's Dictionary*. They looked back. Sparks had ignited the roof; in minutes, only the bank's vault would survive.

The conflagration raged on.

Useless without water.

A desperate attempt to save the town. And a last image of the Sawdust Corner Saloon.

103

Originally captioned,
"Bodie Bill—age 2½ years—
firebug of the Bodie fire."

With his bank and 9 out of 10 Bodie's tinder-dry buildings destroyed,
what more was there for town father J.S. Cain to say or do?

In the end, a town born with a whoop was to die with hardly a whimper.

Bodie, wicked Bodie. Cold-eyed men in black swallow-tailed coats.

But there were others, some small-minded and self-righteous, but most—men, women, and children—warm-hearted, and doing their best to carve a life—a good life—from the mines working Bodie Bluff.

They made nowhere somewhere.

Bodie—to the accompaniment of rattling tin roofs and creaking timbers, the howling desert wind sings of your sagebrush grit and fleeting glory.

Oh, what a time it was...

Acknowledgments

In the wake of Bodie's devastating 1932 fire, banker and landowner J.S. Cain didn't give up on the place. Though he died in 1938, his company retained a watchman to discourage looters, would-be arsonists, and the like—until in 1967 Cain's son-in-law Emil Billeb negotiated a transfer of the *entire intact ghost town* to the state of California. If it wasn't for the Cain family, Bodie would be a forgotten swath of broken glass and tumbled-down walls.

Thanks are due for the folks now preserving and managing Bodie—who as well helped make this book become a reality. They include Brian Cahill, State Park Division Chief for Interpretation & Education; Marilyn Linkem, Sierra District Superintendent; and Josh Heitzmann, Bodie's Supervising Ranger. As well, sincere thanks are due the Bodie Foundation, headed by Brad Sturdivant. Board members David James and Norm Stump aided photographer Will Furman in seeking the faded glory of Bodie rooms and parlors.

Foundation historian Terri Geissinger, with an eye to assuring accuracy, thoughtfully reviewed the book's text.

In addition accuracy was afforded by the recollections and research of Frank Wedertz in his *Bodie: 1859–1900*; by the portrait of the town's stalking badmen in Roger McGrath's *Gunfighters, Highwaymen, & Vigilantes*; by a meticulous account of its mines and mining in Michael Piatt's *Bodie: "The Mines Are Looking Well;"* and by personal histories documented in Nick Gariaeff's *Discovering Bodie*. All are recommended for further reading.

As the Cain family saved the place, others have preserved its historic images. The book is particularly indebted to Wil Jorae of California State Park Photographic Archives in Sacramento, Lee Brumbaugh of the Nevada Historical Society in Reno, and Kent Stoddard of Bridgeport's Mono County Historical Society—as well as the many sources listed in the Photography Credits to follow.

There was frequently a need to repair and enhance often damaged images, with credit due David Meltzer, Chris Pyle, and Molly Bosted.

At Sunbelt Publications, it was as ever a pleasure working with founders and friends Diana and Lowell Lindsay, ever enthusiastic production manager Debi Young, and imaginative graphic designer Kathleen Wise.

And finally, harkening to the past, what of the folks who trod Bodie's boardwalks? Hardworking miners, squint-eyed shootists, brazen strumpets, earnest lawmen, little girls in white dresses with giant bows in their hair. They too are to be thanked. As players in a high desert drama, they left their mark and lent us their stories.

Visiting Bodie, you might pay them a visit, as they rest in peace in the cemetery uphill to the West.

Photography Credits

Contemporary color photographs—including a number of reflecting "Inside-Out" images—are the work of **Will Furman**. Exceptions are credited in the following list (that primarily documents historical images).

Multiple photographs on a page are listed clockwise from upper left (a, b, c, d). If known, photographers and artists are credited in boldface.

1a–3	Author's collection
5	Nevada Historical Society
6a	**Nicholas Clapp**
7	Seaver Center, Los Angeles County Museum
8a, b	Bancroft Library, University of California Library, Berkeley
9a–10	Mono County Historical Society
11a–d	Nevada Historical Society, Billeb Collection
12b	Nevada Historical Society
13a	**Nicholas Clapp**
14b, c	**Nicholas Clapp**
15a	Courtesy of California State Parks, image 090-14764
18a	University of Oregon Library, Andrews Collection
19a	Bodie State Historic Park, Cain Collection
20–22a	Huntington Library
24a	Covina Historical Society, **C.W. Tucker**
24b	Wells Fargo & Company
25a	Mono County Courthouse Archive
28a, b	**Nicholas Clapp**
29b	**Nicholas Clapp**
33	Mono County Historical Society
39a–40	Mono County Historical Society
41a	Getty Images, **Neil Lockhart**
41b	Autry National Center
42a	**Nicholas Clapp**
42b–43	Author's collection
44a	Courtesy of California State Parks, image 090-14592
44b	Getty Images, **Alan Lagadu**
45a–c	**Nicholas Clapp**
49a	**Dave James**
49b–50a	California State Library

Index

The cemetery's mournful "Angel of Bodie."